Original title:
Tropical Oasis of the Soul

Copyright © 2025 Creative Arts Management OÜ
All rights reserved.

Author: Juliana Wentworth
ISBN HARDBACK: 978-1-80581-664-5
ISBN PAPERBACK: 978-1-80581-191-6
ISBN EBOOK: 978-1-80581-664-5

Whispers of Sunlit Shores

The sun giggles on the sand,
Where footprints dance like jolly bands.
Seagulls swoop with comic flair,
Chasing snacks without a care.

A crab in shades struts with pride,
With a sideways swagger, he won't hide.
The waves laugh as they rush and play,
Tickling toes in the sun's bright ray.

Heartbeats Beneath Palm Canopies

Beneath the palms, a ticklish breeze,
Whispers secrets between the trees.
Laughter echoes in the air,
As monkeys play without a care.

A picnic spread with quirky treats,
Sandwiches shaped like funny beats.
The juice spills in a vibrant mess,
And everyone wears a smile, I guess.

Serenity in Swaying Palms

Palm leaves sway like dancers bright,
Swaying left and right, what a sight!
Cricketschirp their evening song,
While the stars join in, all night long.

A hammock flips, then squeaks with joy,
'No more naps for this silly boy!'
The moon just winks, then hides its face,
As laughter fills this breezy space.

The Color of Healing Waters

In waters blue where giggles flow,
Fish tail-bop in a joyful show.
A snorkel flips, a splash and splash,
The sun reflects in a funny flash.

Dive in quick, but watch your toes,
For tickly fins will surely pose!
The bubbles rise in gleeful cheer,
Splashing love in water, here!

Serenity Wrapped in Vibrant Green

Under palm trees swaying low,
Lizards dance in vibrant glow.
Sun-kissed friends with drinks in hand,
They sip from coconuts so grand.

Laughs echo through the leafy dome,
While crabs act like they own the foam.
In shades of green, life feels just right,
As iguanas plan their midnight flight.

The Art of Sipping the Breeze

A breeze that tickles at my nose,
Like tiny fairies in a pose.
Straws in drinks like flowers bloom,
While seagulls plot to steal our zoom.

With laughter bubbling over ice,
Each sip makes the day feel nice.
Coconuts with crazy hats,
Join in on all the silly chats.

Tranquil Songs of the Afternoon

The ocean hums a lullaby,
While flip-flops flop as folks walk by.
Sandcastles rise like dreams at dawn,
But watch out! Here comes a sneaky prawn!

Sunburned noses, laughter loud,
We simply can't blend in that crowd.
With palm tree shades upon our heads,
We serenade the sleeping beds.

Driftwood Dreams on the Beach

Driftwood pieces tell their tales,
While beach balls bounce like little whales.
Tangled hair and salty air,
As kids embark on quests with flair.

Sunset paints the sky with glee,
As we jam to a ukulele spree.
With laughter lined in every grain,
This silly life is ours to gain.

Gentle Whispers of Island Winds

The leaves gossip secrets, oh so sweet,
While crabs dance cha-cha on the warm sand feet.
Palm trees wave hello, doing their best,
In this quirky land, who needs to rest?

The sun wears shades like a cool beach dude,
Ice cream melts fast, oh what a rude mood!
Seagulls squawk jokes that quite seldom land,
In this laughable heat, it's simply unplanned!

Serenity Beneath the Canopy

The jungle has a party, can you hear the beat?
Monkeys in tuxedos, dancing on their feet.
Parrots tell tales of the night's wild fun,
While sloths judge us all, saying, 'Why run?'

Beneath the sprawling trees, mushrooms wear hats,
It's a fashion show, featuring wise old bats.
Every breeze tickles, every branch has glee,
Nature's a comedian, can't you see?

Mirage of the Mind's Battlefield

In the brain's own jungle, confusion is king,
Thoughts chase each other like a crazy spring.
Do I want ice cream or that salad I see?
Battle on the menu, who will win me?

Ideas swing like vines, some twisted and curled,
While daydreams tumble, 'Round and 'round they twirled.

Just grab that coconut, take a swig and pretend,
This merry mirage never has to end!

Reflections of the Sunset Soul

As daylight bids farewell, the colors collide,
A canvas of chaos, nature's wild ride.
The sun winks at us with a fiery grin,
While we trip over sandals, chuckling from within.

The horizon chuckles, a jovial display,
As the sky flips pancakes in a breakfast ballet.
In the glow of the dusk, find joy in the jest,
For laughter and warmth are what we love best!

A Tapestry of Warmth and Wonder

Beneath the sun, a wild parade,
Frogs in sunglasses, unafraid.
Mangoes fall like shooting stars,
While dancing lizards strum guitars.

Palm trees sway with pompous flair,
As crabs play hide-and-seek with air.
Coconuts don their fancy hats,
While joyful parrots chat like brats.

A Haven of Solitude and Wonder

A hammock sways, it's quite the scene,
Bumbly bees in a jittery routine.
Sipping juice with a splash of glee,
While sloths throw shade on a nearby tree.

Fish in flip flops swim with style,
Ignoring the world with a carefree smile.
Crickets throw a late-night bash,
While iguanas join in for a splash.

Fragrance of the Earth Woven with Sky

Banana peels lie everywhere,
As monkeys hop without a care.
Fresh piña colada drips, oh dear,
While butterflies giggle, drinking beer.

The breeze sings softly, tickles the toes,
While laughter trails wherever it goes.
A timid turtle tries to dance,
Stepping on dreams, but taking a chance.

Tales of the Serene Coastline

Waves tell stories with vibrant glee,
As sandcastles giggle at the sea.
A crab pulls pranks, oh what a jest,
While seagulls play "who stole my nest?"

Sunset paints the sky in a swirl,
While dolphins leap and give a twirl.
Under stars, the night begins,
As fireflies join to share our sins.

A Haven Crafted in Green

In the shade, I munch on fruit,
A coconut rolls, too cute to boot.
The parrot laughs, I seek a snack,
He squawks in glee, "Don't hold it back!"

Palm fronds sway, the dance is wild,
A lizard's strut, like an awkward child.
Sunburned dreams in fields so bright,
I trip on roots, oh what a sight!

Starlit Conversations by the Shore

Under stars that wink and blink,
With flavors bold, I try to think.
The waves compete, they crash and laugh,
While crabs engage in a tiny graft.

My drink's too strong, oh what a mix,
The ice says, "Chill!" but I'm in a fix.
A jellyfish floats, it seems so wise,
I blame the punch for my silly sighs.

Beneath the Gaze of Ancient Winds

A whispering breeze, so cheeky and sly,
Tangles my hair, oh! It's not shy.
I chase a kite that takes to the sky,
While a crab rustles by, oh my, oh my!

The trees chuckle with leaves all aglow,
"Catch that banana before it doth go!"
A monkey swings, with quick little feet,
Grabs my snack—now that's quite the feat!

Breath of the Island Breeze

With every gust, a tickle I feel,
Twirling in glee like a crazy wheel.
My sunglasses fly, oh where did they go?
They land on a goat, who steals the show!

The sand is hot beneath my toes,
A friendly crab shows me how to pose.
With laughter and joy filling the air,
This silly escapade has nary a care!

Awe of the Gentle Surf

Waves dance like clumsy dancers,
Twirling and splashing like silly prancers.
Each bubble bursts with a giggle,
While seagulls squawk in a jiggle.

Sand castles rise, then meet their doom,
As kids' laughter fills the room.
The tide teases, pulls them away,
Who knew surf could play all day?

Sanctuary Found in Sands

Beneath the sun, my towel's my throne,
In the kingdom of sand, I'm never alone.
Seashells whisper their salty tales,
While crabs march in their tiny trails.

Flip-flops fly like birds in flight,
Chasing their pairs in a comical sight.
I sip my drink with a little umbrella,
A fruity concoction, oh what a fella!

Cradled in a Coconut's Embrace

A coconut smiles, a fuzzy delight,
Crack it open—what a sight!
Milk spills like laughter all around,
While coconut water's the best ever found.

Inside I ponder, the nutty life,
Do coconuts dream of faraway strife?
They sway to the tune of the breezy air,
All the while grinning without a care.

Celestial Dawn Over Oceanic Dreams

Morning light spills like orange juice,
The horizon's blur—let's cut it loose!
Waves giggle softly at sleepy shores,
While roosters crow like they're on tours.

Bright fish dazzle, all colors combined,
They flash their scales, the ocean's blind.
I whisper to clouds, 'Make a scene!'
As the sun winks, it casts the magical sheen.

The Pulse of Life in the Jungle

In the jungle, where the monkeys play,
My morning coffee's not far away.
Parrots squawking with vibrant flair,
I think they want my breakfast share.

Lizards plotting, with a game to scheme,
They sunbathe while I chase my dream.
Coconut palms sway, wave hello,
With every breeze, my worries go.

The jaguar's trying to steal my snack,
But I just laugh, and watch him hack.
Giraffes gossip, necks intertwined,
Their conversation's hard to find.

In this lively dance of sun and shade,
Happiness blooms, and troubles fade.
Life here is a circus, wild and free,
Join the fun, it's a jubilee!

Silks of Sunset

As sun dips low, the sky's a show,
I sip my juice, in quite the glow.
Piña colada spills on my shirt,
A sticky situation, but it won't hurt.

Flamingos prancing in shimmery hues,
They're stealing my moves, what can I do?
With every dip of the golden ray,
I dance like nobody's watching, hooray!

The beach ball bounces, more like flops,
A seagull laughs, my snack it pops.
Sandy toes and giggles all around,
Wave after wave, life's joy is found.

As day turns night with a wink and cheer,
The stars come out, my drink is here.
So let's toast to laughter, and sunsets grand,
In this cheeky land, let's take a stand!

Threads of Dawn

Morning light weaves through the trees,
My alarm clock shouts, "Time to seize!"
With sleepy eyes and hair a fright,
Coffee's the key to set things right.

The toucans chuckle as I arrive,
In this early hour, we start to thrive.
Rosy hues wrap the sky so tight,
Dancing shadows emerge, what a sight!

Caffeine's kicking in like a boisterous cheer,
The parakeets squawk, "Get in gear!"
Me and my mug, we conquer the morn,
With laughter and smiles, a new day is born.

So embrace each hue as the day unfolds,
Funny little stories are waiting to be told.
In this vibrant charm, I've found my call,
Threads of joy stitch together us all!

Colors That Heal the Spirit

Bright yellows bounce like laughter,
Green giggles sway in trees,
Blue whispers tickle the air,
Red dances with such ease.

Orange paints the cheek of dawn,
Purple sprinkles a wink so sly,
Pink tickles the toes of plants,
Each hue makes a silly sigh.

Dotting paths with joy so spry,
Tiny spots of bouncing light,
The spectrum sings a merry tune,
As we float on dreams so bright.

With every shade, a chuckle flows,
Healing hearts in vibrant spree,
In this land of winking joy,
The spirit leaps, oh, can't you see?

Serene Waters Cradle the Dreamer

Oh, the water's soft embrace,
Like a hug from a fluffy cat,
It twirls and swirls, a bubbly dance,
Splashing smiles where we're at.

Reflecting clouds that trip and fall,
Bubbles giggle, then they burst,
Each droplet whispers silly tales,
In this realm, we quench our thirst.

Canoes that float on silly streams,
Ducklings quack in perfect tune,
A fish wears glasses, quite absurd,
As we drift beneath the moon.

Ripples laugh as they run by,
Carrying dreams that gleam and play,
In this haven, we just float,
On the waves of a sunny day.

Treasure Hidden in the Canopy

Look above and you might see,
A treasure chest made of leaves,
With jewels of laughter, bright and keen,
Amidst the branches, nature weaves.

Squirrels sing and dance around,
As if to guard their leafy gold,
The acorns wink, a secret found,
In stories that the branches told.

Sunbeams sparkle like confetti,
While critters scamper, oh so sly,
Whispers hint, 'There's fun up here!'
As adventure flits on by.

If you climb up high enough,
You'll find life's really quite a jest,
In every bough, a giggle waits,
And nature's heart is truly blessed.

Light Filtering Through Emerald Leaves

Sunlight peeks with mischief's grin,
Tickling leaves as they do sway,
Each beam's a poke, a playful nudge,
In this bright and zesty play.

Shadows dance like silly ghosts,
As branches flirt with the breeze,
Light-spun fairies toss confetti,
While laughter bubbles like teas.

The green is bright, a lively hue,
Inviting joy to join the mix,
Each flicker's like a cheerful jest,
With sunshine in clever tricks.

Clouds gather to join the fun,
Casting shadows, they join the spree,
In this place where laughter gleams,
An emerald stage for you and me.

Symphony of the Singing Jungle

In the jungle, where monkeys swing,
A symphony plays, oh what a thing.
Parrots squawk in curious tones,
While frogs croon, composing moans.

Lizards strut with swagger so fine,
Dancing along the twisting vine.
Laughter erupts, a wild parade,
In this concert, there's no charade.

Coconut trees tap-dance all night,
While crickets chirp with sheer delight.
The rhythm of leaves in a playful sway,
Makes even the sun feel a bit gay.

So grab a seat in this leafy hall,
Where jungle tunes are enjoyed by all.
You'll chuckle, giggle, and sway your soul,
In this crazy tune, you'll find your role.

In the Arms of Vibrant Flora

Flowers bloom in colors so bright,
They joke about their beauty, what a sight!
Petals gossip about the bee,
While giggling leaves wave 'come and see!'

Cacti wear hats, spiky but chill,
While daisies throw shade, giving a thrill.
Roses blush, they act so coy,
In this garden, there's endless joy.

Vines dangle down, playing leapfrog,
While orchids join in, a lovely dialogue.
Bumblebees buzz with comedic flair,
Tickling blooms with pollen to spare.

So find your joy in this flowery embrace,
Where laughter blooms in every space.
In the arms of blossoms, you'll find a scheme,
That life is but a whimsical dream.

Flight of the Wanderlust Spirit

The birds in flight sing silly songs,
While daring dreams of where one belongs.
They flap and flop with such happy glee,
As they search for a branch or a friendly tree.

Squirrels cheer for a race in the air,
Chasing one another without a care.
Daredevil ants join the wild chase,
As they march on picnic crumbs in joyful haste.

Clouds drift along with puffy high hats,
Winking at kites and playful cats.
The wind whispers tales of places afar,
Enticing hearts beneath the bright star.

So take to the skies and let laughter soar,
With the wanderlust spirit, there's always more.
In the flight of joy, find your zest,
The world's a stage; go be your best!

They Whisper Beneath the Banyan

Beneath the banyan, secrets unfold,
Where leaves share stories, both new and old.
Whispers of wind tickle the day,
As shadows cavort in a mischievous play.

Lizards gossip with quite the flair,
While ants parade on a combative dare.
The banyan grins, a wise old sage,
With laughter echoing through every page.

In the branches, squirrels crack jokes,
While the breeze joins with delightful pokes.
And when the shadows stretch long and wide,
The banyan giggles, with worlds inside.

So let your troubles drift away,
Join the laughter beneath the sway.
In this haven where joy takes a stand,
You'll find a giggle and a helping hand.

Embracing the Aroma of Rain

Puddles splash like happy secrets,
Dancing droplets serenade the ground.
Umbrellas sprout like mushrooms,
As laughter meets the liquid sound.

Rubber boots are stepping stones,
In this joyous, wet parade.
Sipping cocoa with the raindrops,
In our soggy escapade.

The clouds wear silly grins above,
Dressing the day in a cozy quilt.
Our playful hearts in sync,
With every splash, a new thrill built.

So we twirl like giggling leaves,
As rainbows arc, a playful tease.
In the scent of fresh-swept earth,
We find our simple, joyful ease.

Serenity Interwoven with the Waves

Waves flirt like a dolphin's smile,
Splashes giggle on the sand.
Surfers chase their foamy dreams,
While seagulls plot to steal our fries.

Beach chairs lean like lazy friends,
Sunbathers with their shades askew.
Sandy toes wiggle with delight,
As laughter dances in the blue.

Coconut drinks with silly straws,
Every sip a burst of cheer.
The surf sings songs of playful joy,
While sunsets paint our hearts sincere.

We build our castles, only to laugh,
As waves come in to knock them down.
Yet every tumble, every fall,
Turns into laughter all around.

Voices of the Breeze at Twilight

Whispers float like feathery dreams,
Through the branches, soft and light.
The moon giggles, peeking through,
As fireflies join the ecstatic flight.

Crickets strum a nighttime tune,
While shadows dance in cheeky jest.
Under starlit, winking skies,
Nature hosts its grandest fest.

The leaves gossip in hushed tones,
Trading secrets with the night.
Petals twirl in secret dances,
In the glow of soft twilight.

And as we sway to the breeze,
A symphony of giggles sings.
Together we embrace the night,
As joy in every rustle springs.

Whimsy in the Heart of Nature's Arms

Bouncing bunnies wear their hats,
While squirrels throw acorn balls.
A wise old tree tells silly tales,
Of rubber ducks and milkshake calls.

Butterflies boast of their wild style,
As flowers blush in vibrant glee.
A sunny day of funny faces,
Paints nature as our jubilee.

Grass tickles toes in giggly sways,
While shadows play hide-and-seek.
Every chirp and every rustle,
Makes us laugh until we squeak.

In this haven, filled with cheer,
Kindred spirits frolic and play.
Whimsy wraps us in its arms,
Where giggles turn the world to sway.

An Elysium Brought to Life

In a land where coconuts smile,
Palm trees dance in a silly style.
With flip-flops flapping, we take flight,
Finding joy from morning 'til night.

Squirrels in shades chase after flies,
A toucan whispers, oh how it tries!
We sip on drinks with umbrellas so bright,
And laughter echoes in the fading light.

Fish in shorts swim, thinking they're cool,
While turtles take a dip in the pool.
Sunburned tourists forget where they parked,
As nature's jokes leave everyone sparkled.

A hammock's calling, it steals the day,
While monkeys plot in a mischievous way.
Forget your worries, they're on the shelf,
Join the fun and just be yourself!

The Calm of Whispering Waves

The waves have secrets, they giggle and sigh,
As seagulls dressed in tuxes swoop by.
Flippers splashing while dolphins do tricks,
All under the sun, life's playful mix.

Starfish wear hats, seashells parade,
Each little creature in nature's charade.
Forget for a moment your worries, my friend,
In this hideaway where smiles never end.

Jellyfish bobbing like clumsy balloons,
Breezes whispering cheerful cartoons.
Sandcastles topple, but never mind,
For the laughter of waves is the best kind.

With each swish, the ocean seems to say,
"Forget the frown, let's party today!"
So join in the fun, toss your cares away,
In the calm where the playful waves sway.

Dappled Sunlight on the Shore

Sunlight dances on the water's skin,
As crabs in tuxedos dance with a grin.
Sandy toes tickle as we walk by,
With flip-flops flying, oh my, oh my!

The beach ball bounces, then takes a leap,
Into the hands of a kid, oh so deep.
Seashells whisper their secrets so sweet,
While kids dig holes with sand toys at their feet.

With laughter and giggles, we build a throne,
Out of driftwood and seashells we've known.
A soundtrack of seagulls, a cheeky choir,
Makes this sunny adventure never tire.

So here's to the fun, to laughter and cheer,
To dappled sunlight that draws us near.
In this sandy paradise, we play and explore,
Chasing squeaky beach toys and asking for more!

Palette of Nature's Abode

Colors splash like paint from a dream,
With flowers that whistle and giggle, it seems.
Butterflies flutter in dazzling display,
As nature orchestrates a colorful play.

Giggling blooms in a sunny parade,
While frogs in tuxedos serenade.
Each hue tells a joke, bright and bold,
In this garden of laughter, treasures unfold.

The breeze tickles leaves, making them sway,
As the sun sets softly on the end of the day.
Bumblebees buzzing with silly cheer,
In this masterpiece, there's nothing to fear.

So come, take part in this whimsical show,
Where humor and color make spirits glow.
In a world painted bright with giggles around,
Nature's abode is where joy can be found!

Swayed by the Rhythm of Nature

In the breeze, my hair's a mess,
Nature's dance, I must confess.
Lizards groove, they lead the way,
Swaying limbs in bright array.

The parrot's squawk, a loud refrain,
Jumps and giggles, what a gain!
Coconuts drop with perfect aim,
Who knew they played this wild game?

The sun in shades of lemon drop,
While banana peels make me flop!
Grasshoppers chirp, a comic tune,
Nature's jesters, afternoon.

With each twist, I lose my feet,
Trip on roots, but feel the beat.
Laughing leaves, they chime along,
Life's a party, can't go wrong!

The Calm After the Storm

After thunder, things go still,
With drenched leaves, a funny thrill.
Rainbows laugh in colors bright,
Nature's way of feeling light.

Puddles form like mini lakes,
Splashing through, the laughter shakes.
Frogs on lily pads, they cheer,
"Join us here, no need to fear!"

What a sight, a squirrel's dash,
Kicking mud, oh what a splash!
Drying hugs from gentle sun,
Those soaked socks? It's all in fun.

So here's to storms that bring delight,
With every drip, the world feels right.
Giggles echo, breezy song,
In nature's play, we all belong!

Embrace of the Silk-Skinned Moon

The moon's a silver, pulpy fruit,
In the sky, it struts its loot.
Stars twinkle, playing peek-a-boo,
While crickets sing their nightly boo-hoo.

I waltz with shadows, twirl and spin,
Underneath the moon's sly grin.
Beneath this glow, the trees take flight,
In comical shapes, what a sight!

A firefly's dance, a tiny rave,
Flickering joy, oh how they behave!
With every blink, their laughter shows,
Teaching me how the fun still grows.

So raise a glass to moonlit glee,
With friends in shadows, wild and free.
Life's a jest under starlit run,
With each embrace, we find our fun!

Blossoms in the Mist of Paradise

Petals shower like confetti, bright,
In this garden, oh what a sight!
Butterflies flutter in a dizzy swirl,
Who knew flowers had such a twirl?

Bees are buzzing, humming a tune,
Chasing pollen 'round the noon.
With their dance, they form a line,
Crashing blooms, they're oh-so-fine!

In the mist, the sun's a tease,
Morning giggles through the trees.
Colors clash like a vibrant brawl,
In this patch, we've got it all.

So let's embrace this floral jest,
With laughs and blooms, we're truly blessed.
In paradise, let heartbeats race,
With every laugh, we find our space!

The Call of the Coral Coast

Beneath a sky so bright and blue,
The seagulls squawk a laughing tune.
With sandy toes and coconut hats,
The sun tan lines are where it's at!

The waves they dance with silly glee,
As fishy friends join in the spree.
A crab in shades, he struts about,
While beach balls bounce and kids all shout!

A salty breeze, a mango treat,
Sunburned noses can't be beat.
We build our castles, tall and wide,
And then we watch as they collide!

Oh, this is life, let's shout and cheer,
In coral coast, we have no fear.
So come and join this wacky bash,
We'll trade our shells for laughs and cash!

Inkling of the Island's Heart

On this isle, a coconut falls,
And everyone inside it brawls.
With pineapples wearing silly hats,
And smooth-talking lizards, how 'bout that?

The palm trees sway in quirky styles,
Their hula-hooping brings us smiles.
Mango shakes with silly straws,
We sip and giggle, just because!

At sunset's glow, the crickets sing,
With karaoke from a frog, the king!
A duck in shades joins in the fray,
As fireflies dance and softly sway.

Island life is one big joke,
With laughter wrapped in every stroke.
So grab a drink, let worries part,
Here beats the rhythm of the heart!

Hues of the Solstice Breeze

In hues of gold and turquoise blue,
The parrots chatter, say it's true.
With dancing feet and carefree spins,
The party starts where the fun begins!

The sun dips low; oh what a sight,
A dancing octopus steals the night.
With glitterfish and jellybean stars,
Our laughter echoes from near to far!

The hammock sways, a sleepy pit,
But wait—did that iguana just quit?
With flip-flops flying and jokes on ice,
Our souls are light, just like a slice!

Under the moon, we strike a pose,
Life's a stage where anything goes.
So let's embrace this silly tease,
In shades of joy and mismatched pleas!

Watercolor Dreams of Dusk

As dusk approaches, colors blend,
A watermelon cheers, my fruity friend!
With stark blue waves and laughter loud,
We paint the night, and draw a crowd!

A dolphin leaps with style and grace,
While everyone wears a giant face.
With glow sticks twirling, what a scene,
The funniest party you've ever seen!

Our beach bonfire crackles bright,
S'mores with fish? That's quite a bite!
Marshmallow dances, what a thrill,
So much joy, it gives a chill!

We'll paint the stars, make wishes bold,
Each memory a treasure to hold.
With giggles and dreams in a cluster,
This night is filled with happy fluster!

Crescendo of Paradise Found

Sipping drinks with tiny umbrellas,
I wore my best grass skirt today,
The parrots laugh, they're great at jokes,
I'm just here hoping they'll pay.

The sand tickles my toes with glee,
While a crab scuttles past with a dance,
I challenge him to a race, oh please!
He huffs and puffs, gives me a glance.

Sunburned noses, oh what a sight,
Lava lamps twinkle in the night,
Coconuts rolling down the beach,
Even the waves have a funny speech!

With laughter echoing through the palms,
I've lost my flip-flops - they've gone rogue,
Under the stars, we sing our psalms,
In this paradise, we will not bogue.

Secrets Shared Beneath the Stars

Under the moon, the secrets flow,
I spilled my dreams, didn't mean to show,
Lying here on this sandy bed,
The fish are giggling, what have I said?

Starfish eavesdrop, they're quite the spies,
They whisper tales of love and fries,
The ocean joins in, an echo of fun,
While the crabs dance under the shimmering sun.

"Tell me more," the seagulls cry,
As I share my wishes, oh my oh my,
They drop their chips, forget the game,
Chortling loudly, they'll never be tame.

The night drips laughter like honey sweet,
In this secret spot where mischief meets,
Each chuckle shared a melody bright,
Beneath the stars, everything feels right.

When Dreams Sail to the Horizon

I set my dreams adrift on a boat,
With sunscreen, snacks, and a goat to gloat,
The horizon calls, a joyous yell,
But my goat thinks it's a fancy hotel!

The waves are waltzing, quite a delight,
A whale winks at me, oh what a sight,
I shout, "Hey, buddy, come join the fun!"
He does a backflip, then promptly runs.

Pineapple hats float in the sun's embrace,
While my dreams try too hard to keep pace,
I laugh as they fumble, trip and fall,
Who knew ambition could be so small?

With every wave, a giggle is cast,
Sailing toward futures, just having a blast,
From whispers of hope, my heart takes flight,
As dreams sail forth, all feels just right.

A Refuge in the Heart of Wilderness

In the wild, we build a fort of leaves,
With laughter loud enough to make thieves,
The raccoons gather, they're ready to play,
We'll host a party, no time to delay!

Bees buzzing tunes, they whistle the beat,
While squirrels debate on who's got the sweet,
With berries galore, we feast like kings,
Nature's buffet serves the best of things.

The sun sets low, an orange parade,
We roast marshmallows, and sing unafraid,
A raccoon DJ, spinning the night,
We dance under stars, everything's bright.

In this wild nook, I've found my home,
With laughter and friends, I'll never roam,
As dreams mingle with each rustling leaf,
A crazy refuge, beyond belief!

Rhapsody of Tides at Dusk

Waves whisper secrets, oh so bright,
Crabs dance like they own the night.
Flamingos wearing shades of pink,
Laughing at the drinks they clink.

Coconuts juggle in the breeze,
Monkeys swinging from the trees.
Sandcastles rise, then fall like fate,
While turtles contemplate their plate.

Seagulls squawk, a chatty crew,
As beach balls chase the sun's debut.
The tide comes in, a silly race,
Splashing dreams all over the place.

We close our eyes, breathe in the fun,
Tomorrow brings more rays and sun.
In this crazy paradise we play,
Wishing we could live this way!

Luminous Reflections on Sandy Shores

Under moons that glow like lightbulbs bright,
Starfish posing, what a curious sight.
With surfboards stacked high on the sand,
We laugh till we can't make a stand.

Sand drifts in with a cheeky grin,
A crab ambush might soon begin.
Laughter bubbles like fizzy drinks,
As dolphins dance, oh how it winks!

Seashells gossip of salty dreams,
While the horizon holds moonlit beams.
Flip-flops flipping, giggles arise,
Under the blanket of starlit skies.

With frosty treats and sandy toes,
A parade of friends and funny shows.
Tonight's a whirlwind of silly delight,
As we sip our punch and toast to the night!

The Heartbeat of the Island

Palms sway like they're in a groove,
As parrots shimmy, ooh, watch them move!
Rhythms drum from the beachy crowd,
Making memories that feel so loud.

Sunsets splash colors, red and gold,
Drawing shadows, both timid and bold.
We chase our thoughts in flip-flop bliss,
With every wave, there's magic to kiss.

In the kitchen, a blender's roar,
With mango smoothies, who could ask for more?
Bananas flying through the air,
As laughter lingers everywhere.

The ukulele sings soft and sweet,
While fireflies dance to the beat.
Heartbeat of this merry land,
Keeps us smiling, hand in hand!

Secrets of the Shimmering Lagoon

Bubbles rise with a pop and a twist,
Mermaids giggle as they lovingly assist.
Fish in tuxedos do their parade,
In this lagoon, where fun's homemade.

Snorkels clash in a curious race,
With laughter echoing through the space.
Marshmallow boats bob like fluffy dreams,
As locals fish for silly memes.

Jellyfish waltz, their tentacles sway,
While sunbathers muse, 'What a day!'
Fruit floats teasing taste buds to play,
In a never-ending fiesta display.

As twilight brings a hint of strange,
We dive into laughter, never change.
Secrets of the lagoon unfold,
With every ripple, new tales told!

Embrace of the Coconut Grove

In the grove of coconuts, laughter sways,
Monkeys swing wildly, in silly plays.
Beneath the palms, we dance with glee,
Sipping juice, as happy as can be.

The hermit crab is a master of flair,
Wearing a shell that's beyond compare.
He struts his stuff like a tiny star,
While we cheer him on, not caring how far.

With sand between our toes, we giggle and shout,
Building castles that'll all wash out.
But who needs dreams made of ocean foam?
When laughter's our treasure, we're right at home.

So raise your coconuts, let's toast to fun,
In this paradise, our laughter's never done.
Under the sun, we find our reprieve,
In this grove of joy, we truly believe.

Elixir of the Island Heart

The sun sets low, a golden surprise,
As we mix drinks with questionable ties.
A splash of laughter, a pinch of mirth,
Tasting the nectar of our island birth.

With every sip, we spill a bit,
On our goofy dance, we'll never quit.
Parrots squawk, joining our song,
In this merry chaos, we all belong.

Our island hearts beat like a drum,
To rhythms silly, and feeling numb.
The beach is our stage, with only one act,
Tripping on sand, it's a matter of fact.

So let's raise our glasses to mishaps galore,
A toast to the laughter that we all adore.
In this crazy mix, we find our part,
Sipping elixirs straight from the heart.

Magic Beneath the Starry Sky

Under a blanket of glimmering lights,
We share our stories of curious sights.
The stars above wink as we play,
While fireflies dance in a silly ballet.

The moon's our friend, with a cheeky grin,
As we holler jokes that make our heads spin.
A sea turtle sneaks by, with a wink,
I swear he's judging, but what do you think?

We race the waves, shout loud and proud,
Our island laughter creates a crowd.
In the glow of night, our dreams take flight,
Chasing our shadows until morning light.

So here's to magic, to giggles and cheer,
To memories made that we hold so dear.
Beneath this sky, we find our way,
In this silly dance, we forever stay.

Pathways Through Emerald Canopies

Wandering pathways where the sun peeks through,
The jungle giggles in fresh morning dew.
We stumble and trip, but hey, who's keeping score?
Every branch overhead has a secret to explore.

A parrot shouts, "You call that a strut?!"
As we chase our feet, and dance like a nut.
Each twig a stage, each leaf a line,
In the forest's embrace, our spirits align.

The monkeys point as we hit a vine,
Swinging like pros, looking wholly divine.
But when we fall, we all burst out loud,
In this crazy adventure, we're always proud.

So let's wander these paths, with hearts so light,
In this emerald world, everything feels right.
With every silly step through the trees we trod,
We savor this laughter, a gift from the gods.

Footprints on the Soft Earth

In the sand, my feet leave trails,
Like a clumsy dance, I must prevail.
With each step, it's quite absurd,
I spot a crab, oh what a nerd!

Waves tease my toes, splash and play,
I say, "Stop it!" but they won't sway.
A seagull swoops, eyeing my fries,
I toss them back, to my surprise!

Barefoot antics, laughter's found,
A hidden gem beneath the ground.
Coconuts laugh, they roll away,
Oh dear, let's make this a game today!

So here I stand, mud on my face,
In this silly, joyous place.
For every slip and every fall,
Are the footprints of my heart, after all.

The Soul's Journey Through Lush Growth

In jungles thick, I take a stride,
Where vines twist tales of joy and pride.
A monkey leaps, he grins at me,
"Don't be a sapling, come climb a tree!"

Tickling leaves whisper in jest,
They plan surprise parties, oh what a quest!
I dance with flowers, quick on my feet,
Each bloom a laughter, sweet and neat.

The sun peeks through on a sunny jest,
"Get out of my rays!" I can't rest.
A parrot squawks, loud as can be,
He's got opinions about my tea!

Yet, in this bounteous, lively throng,
My spirit hums, it sings a song.
With silly moments stitched so tight,
This growth is sheer delight and light!

Resplendent Awakenings in the Wilds

Each dawn, the sun pops up so bright,
The chattering critters take their flight.
A bear yawns wide, spills his dreams,
"I'm late for breakfast!" Oh, how it seems!

Bamboo shakes like a maraca's cheer,
Echoed laughter fills the atmosphere.
A sloth waves slow, he's in no rush,
I'm tempted to join, but oh, the hush!

Colorful birds flaunt their attire,
A peacock struts, the spotlight's fire.
He winks at blooms in vibrant hues,
"Life's a parade! Wear your best shoes!"

So in this wild, wacky playground,
Emotions whirl, twirl all around.
My heart's a canvas, splashed in fun,
With every sunrise, we all run!

Tides of Emotion Gently Flowing

Waves of giggles lap at the shore,
With every swell, I love them more.
A dolphin leaps, he gives a grin,
"Come ride the waves, let the fun begin!"

By the tide, seaweed makes a crown,
I don it proudly, without a frown.
A fish flips by, curious and sly,
He nudges, "You're strange!" with a wink of an eye.

Winds of whimsy whistle their tune,
While crabs host parties in the afternoon.
With shells as hats and sand as cake,
I join the fun, for goodness' sake!

So, let the waves roll on and play,
In this salty joy, I'll always stay.
For every tide that pulls and flows,
Brings endless laughter where the heart glows!

Lullabies of the Gentle Breeze

In the hammock, I sway so slow,
My feet up high, like a wiggly toe.
A parrot squawks, 'Time to shake!'
I mumble back, 'Don't make a mistake.'

Palm leaves rustle their secret tune,
As I dream of lunch; I'm missing a boon.
Coconut drinks are calling my name,
But the ice says, 'You can't win this game!'

Sand crabs dance in a wobbly line,
They pinch my toe, what a weird sign!
With every step, they scurry away,
Laughing at me in their crabby ballet!

So here I nap, in this funny heat,
Where even the lizards admit defeat.
In my bliss, I shall not complain,
'Cause tomorrow, I'll do this again!'

Sanctuary of Colorful Feathers

A flock of birds painted like rain,
They squawk and crack, creating a strain.
One's got a hat made of bright lime,
Laughing out loud, it's plumage prime!

Fluffy friends on the wire above,
Charming away in a squawking love.
They argue about who sings the best,
While I sip juice, taking my rest.

A butterfly wiggles its fancy dress,
Leaves my daydream in a frilly mess.
"What's your name?" I ask with a grin,
It changes colors—no clue where to begin!

So I join this party, feeling so bright,
With laughter and joy, it feels just right.
Nature's jesters, they steal the show,
In this wild place of color and glow!

Enchanted Shores of Serenity

Waves crash in, with a friendly shout,
They tickle my toes, making me pout.
A sandcastle pops up, wearing a crown,
Till a seagull swoops and tears it down!

The tide retreats with a cheeky wave,
Leaving behind treasures it gave.
A flip-flop floats by, dancing away,
While I sit here, pondering my play.

A beach ball bounces, oh what a sight,
It rolls past a crab, who's ready to bite.
The sun beams down, giving me cheer,
With shades on, the world seems so near!

As I laugh at the antics around,
Joy and silliness in every sound.
In this haven where giggles resound,
I wave to the wind, spinning round and round!

Harmony in the Shade of Mango Trees

Beneath green canopies, I find my throne,
Where all the fruits of summer have grown.
A mango drops, right on my hat,
I feel like a king and the world is my mat!

The ants hold parades, oh what a sight,
Gathering crumbs in a march of delight.
They stop for a sip from a puddly gleam,
Belly flops only in ants' silly dream!

The breeze brings whispers of secrets profound,
As I chuckle at squirrels hopping around.
They're arguing who gets the last snack,
And I just smile, hoping they won't attack!

So here I lounge, with laughter and cheer,
In this leafy place where joy's crystal clear.
The sun fades gently, my heart's quite full,
In this sunny kingdom, all feels quite cool!

Reflections of a Wanderer's Heart

A wanderer strolled by the sea,
Chasing crabs as fast as can be.
Flip-flops flying, oh what a sight,
Falling face-first like a kite in flight.

A parrot squawks, 'Hey, what gives?'
The wanderer laughs, 'I just live!'
Sunburned nose and a sack of snacks,
In search of fish that totally lacks.

With coconuts scattered, quite absurd,
He trips on a shell, oh how he stirred!
The waves giggle, with mischief abound,
As he throws a dance on the sandy ground.

But in the chaos, he's found his cheer,
A sunlit heart, with no room for fear.
In every stumble, a song will arise,
To chase the clouds and touch the skies.

The Quietude of the Tropics

In the hush of the palms, a sloth yawns,
Wearing sunglasses and festive brawn.
He sips on nectar with such slow grace,
Taking his time, no frantic race.

A monkey swings by with a cheeky grin,
'Why hurry, friend? Let the fun begin!'
With a banana hat, he leaps with flair,
Creating laughter that dances in air.

The iguanas lounge, all zen and calm,
Practicing yoga, with a twist and balm.
While the breeze whispers secrets, so sly,
Invite the night to let worries fly.

In this serene, delightful show,
Time's just a joke, it moves nice and slow.
With laughter echoing through lush green trees,
Finding peace means just a gentle tease.

Vows Made Under the Coconut Palms

Beneath the palms, two hearts entwine,
With a fruity drink, they sip and dine.
'I'll love you more than this piña colada,
Even when you're a bit of a stada!'

He kneels with a ring made of seaweed strands,
She laughs so hard, she drops her hands.
'In storms or sun, I'll stick like glue,'
'And never steal your fries, it's true!'

Together they giggle, in vows they swim,
'We'll dance with the crabs and on a whim.
If you trip on a shell, I'll catch your fall,
And spread laughter like confetti to all!'

As the sun sets low, a raucous crowd,
Their love shines bright, humor unbowed.
With coconut dreams and a cheer so swell,
They seal their bond in a chuckling spell.

Rushing Water Meets the Stillness Within

A river rushes with a playful roar,
Splashing stones with a giggle galore.
While pondering fish, with bubbles that rise,
Swirling in laughter under the skies.

There swims a frog in a jazzy cap,
Croaking old songs, a wise little chap.
'Why glide on by, when you can just play?
Join me in laughter, throw worries away!'

As waves frolic and dance in their glee,
The world feels lighter, as light should be.
With each splash of joy, the heart learns to blend,
In the comedy nature always intends.

So let the current lead to the shore,
Where laughter echoes forevermore.
In this wild rhythm, both rush and still,
A whimsical dance, a soul's sweet thrill.

Vignettes of Tranquil Shores

On a beach where the sun likes to glare,
Lizards wiggle without a care.
Seagulls steal chips with a squawk,
While I sunbathe and hope they mock.

Waves giggle as they dance on the sand,
I try to build castles, but they're not so grand.
Crabs in tuxedos plotting a feast,
But I'm still here, munching on yeast.

Drinks with umbrellas, oh what a sight,
My coconut's got more flair than my bite.
Palm trees sway, gossiping low,
"Did you see that guy? He is quite the show."

A nap on the shore, is that a wise plan?
Maybe not, but hey, I'm a fan!
In the breeze, life's just a jest,
Waves whispering, "You're truly blessed."

Harmony Between Sky and Sea

Clouds are fluff, like cotton candy dreams,
I paddle my boat, or so it seems.
Frogs on lily pads snicker and chat,
As I try to catch a fancy hat.

The ocean sings tunes of a silly sort,
Fish in bowties hold a court.
With a splash and a giggle, they dart away,
Leaving me here, in a watery ballet.

Sunset spills orange on the gleaming blue,
I wave to the dolphins, oh, if they only knew.
Turtles in flip-flops join the parade,
"Let's all celebrate the sunshine we've made!"

Stars emerge, a twinkling jest,
While I fumble for snacks that I've blessed.
In this realm where laughter flows,
The sky and sea put on their shows.

A Garden of Thoughts in Blossom

In a garden of whims, where ideas sprout,
A bee and a butterfly dance about.
Thoughts like flowers, blooming in rows,
Smile at the sun, while the breeze gently blows.

Daisies argue about who's the best,
While the daisies try to outshine the rest.
"Petals are pretty!" they buzz and hum,
But I just laugh, oh what a fun!

Vegetables plot to join the fun,
"I'll be the salad!" says one, oh what a pun!
Herbs are the gossip, they know all the news,
"Did you hear what happened to the poor old prune?"

Underneath it all, a joy blooms bright,
In the garden of thoughts, everything's light.
With each tiny giggle, the roots dig deep,
Where laughter is planted, joy grows to keep.

Meditations on the Edge of the Water

Sitting where ripples tickle my toes,
A fish looks up and gives me a pose.
I meditate, watching clouds drift by,
All while avoiding that pesky fly.

Waves whisper secrets, "Don't take it too stiff,"
As I try to balance on this drifting gift.
Nature's a comedian, having some fun,
With me as the punchline, oh, how I run!

The pelicans dive, like they own the place,
Snatching fish like they're in a race.
I cheer them on, waving my hands,
"Go get that snack, flip over the lands!"

As sunset paints the sky in delight,
I wonder if seagulls have a good night.
With laughter around me, I feel alive,
At the edge of the water, where silliness thrives.

Beneath the Veil of Exotic Blooms

In fields where colors play and tease,
The blooms are laughing in the breeze.
With petals wide and scents like cake,
They sway and giggle, make no mistake.

A butterfly lands with a wink,
On a flower pot that's lost its drink.
"Hey buddy, share that nectar sweet!"
The flower says with a funny tweet.

A squirrel's got moves like he's in a show,
Practicing for the tree-top glow.
But trip he did, oh what a sight!
Fell in a daisy—such a delight!

The sun sets low, it starts to fade,
While laughter lingers in the glade.
In this garden full of cheer,
Every day's a carnival here!

Sun-Kissed Dreams on Quiet Beaches

A crab in shades, he struts with flair,
Riding waves without a care.
He nods to shells, they giggle loud,
As seagulls dive swooping 'round the crowd.

The sun loungers know how to chill,
While beach balls bounce, giving a thrill.
A kid takes aim, throws with glee,
But lands the ball right on a bee!

The lifeguard snores in a tall chair,
Oblivious to the sandy affair.
As waves crash down, the laughter erupts,
In this sandy circus where joy erupts.

When twilight paints the sky so bright,
Jellyfish glow like stars at night.
With flip-flops flying, all take a bow,
In a sun-kissed show, they're shining now!

Melodies of the Mystic Mangroves

In tangled roots where shadows lurk,
The crickets chirp, they love to work.
A parrot jokes, "Squawk, what's the plan?"
Echoes dance, laugh like a band!

A fish jumps up, attempts a song,
Splashing notes that don't last long.
"Try again!" the frogs all croak,
As reeds hum back, it's quite the joke!

A monkey swings with a playful yell,
Grabs a coconut, but oh, what a spill!
His buddies chuckle, "What a miss!"
He grins and swings, "Just one more kiss!"

Dusk arrives with stars so bright,
The mangroves chuckle, just pure delight.
While fireflies waltz in a gentle sway,
The night wraps up the games of the day!

The Dance of the Firefly

In the night where shadows play,
Tiny lanterns twinkle away.
They flit and frolic, a lively crew,
Each little glow with a giggle, too.

A firefly trips on a leaf so grand,
"I'm not clumsy!" he says, tries to stand.
His buddies laugh, they light up the dark,
With a glowing dance, they leave their mark.

The moon beams down, a shining stage,
While frogs join in with rhymes of sage.
"Ribbit, ribbit, come and see,
A firefly circus, all for free!"

As dawn approaches, the show slows down,
With sleepy smiles, no frown in town.
In the soft light, they wink goodbye,
Promising fun when night's nigh high!

Spirit of the Cacao Blossom

In a land where the chocolates grow,
The flowers giggle, putting on a show.
Buzzing bees dance with glee,
While cocoa beans sip on sweet tea.

Monkeys wear hats as they swing by,
Telling jokes that make the toucans cry.
Chocolate rivers flow, oh what a treat,
Even the ants have a dance with their feet.

Rain clouds gather, don't bring a frown,
For puddles are chocolate, let's all splash down!
Marshmallow clouds float high above,
In this sweet haven, we laugh with love.

So raise your cocoa cups up high,
Cheers to the laughter that flutters and flies.
In this land full of giggles and grace,
We'll snack on joy at a chocolate pace.

Whispers of the Palms

Palm trees lean in with giggles and sighs,
Swapping stories of sunny, bright skies.
Swaying their fronds, they start a big cheer,
As the cicadas join in the symphonic sphere.

A parrot in shades is life of the party,
Reminding us all to be a bit hearty.
Swinging from branches, the monkeys yell loud,
"Who else loves to dance? Come join our crowd!"

The coconuts chuckle as they roll on the ground,
While crabs play limbo in the warm, sandy round.
Flip-flopping around, we join in the fun,
This paradise hums, the laughter's begun!

Under the palms, the air's filled with glee,
We toast with our drinks, just you and me.
So let's sway with the breeze, let our worries fall,
In the land where the palms brighten us all.

Sanctuary Beneath the Canopy

Beneath the branches, the sunshine plays,
With shadows that dance in playful ways.
Lizards in sunglasses strut with pride,
While gummy bears have a fun-filled ride.

The breeze whispers secrets to trees so wise,
As squirrels trade jokes and wear funny ties.
Bamboo shoots giggle, leaning to chat,
It's a vibrant place, imagine that!

The butterflies flutter, hold a beauty parade,
In vibrant colors, they waltz and cascade.
A sloth takes a nap, oh what a sight,
Dreaming of bananas, oh what a delight!

In this green wonder, laughter's the key,
Join in the mirth, let your heart feel free.
For nestled here, in nature's embrace,
Is a sanctuary where we all find our place.

Echoes of Sunlit Waters

By the lagoon where the sunbeams play,
Frogs wear top hats and leap through the fray.
The fish hum tunes as they swim in a line,
While ducks start a show, oh wouldn't that be fine?

Splashing about, the herons take flight,
In synchronized moves, what a funny sight!
Little turtles gossip as they sun on a rock,
Making funny faces at the big tick-tock.

Ripples of laughter weave through the air,
As the water's reflections show joy everywhere.
Even the raindrops join in the fun,
Dancing on lily pads, oh, aren't we all one?

So here by the waters, laughter is free,
A world full of whimsy, just you and me.
Let's ride the waves of this joyous sound,
In echoes of laughter, forever we're found.

www.ingramcontent.com/pod-product-compliance
Lightning Source LLC
Chambersburg PA
CBHW072122070526
44585CB00016B/1530